CASEY'S CASE

David Rish
Illustrated by Margaret Power

For Liam, Robert and Nicholas

Written by David Rish
Illustrated by Margaret Power
Designed by Peter Shaw

Published by Mimosa Publications Pty Ltd
PO Box 779, Hawthorn 3122, Australia
© 1995 Mimosa Publications Pty Ltd
All rights reserved

Distributed in the United Kingdom by
Kingscourt Publishing Limited
PO Box 1427, London W6 9BR, England

Distributed in Australia by
Rigby Heinemann
(a division of Reed International Books Australia Pty Ltd)
22 Salmon Street, Port Melbourne, Victoria 3207

Distributed in New Zealand by
Shortland Publications Limited
2B Cawley Street, Ellerslie, Auckland

03 02 01 00 99 98
10 9 8 7 6 5 4 3
Printed in Hong Kong through Bookbuilders Ltd

ISBN 0 7327 1560 1

CONTENTS

1 Unpacking 5

2 Joker in the Pack 11

3 Backpacking 19

4 Trapped! 29

5 Cross Words 37

6 Crossed Flags 45

7 Crossed Wires? 57

8 Crossing the Line 65

9 An Open-and-shut Case 75

Epilogue The Case Is Closed 91

Unpacking

My short career as a detective began in Halls, a small town where my father had taken a job with the Halls Corporation. The Corporation had been started by a famous but solitary inventor, E. Henry Halls, who seemed to be something of a mystery. It was rumoured that he'd gone completely mad, his brain turned by all the hard work involved in creating his many inventions.

Dad's a mathematician, a brilliant one, which was why the Halls Corporation had offered him a job working on a top-secret rocket project. My grandparents were visiting us when the letter offering the position arrived, so Dad left me in their capable hands while he flew off for an interview.

Two days later, they drove me out to the airport to meet his plane. Dad came down the walkway bubbling with excitement. "The town's great, Case," he said. "I've found the perfect flat, with a good school nearby, and (please note my brilliant pun) the salary is *astronomical*."

Grandma and Grandpa and I laughed, mostly because Dad seemed so happy. My father hasn't been really happy since my mother died. For the last four years he's gone from job to job, calling himself a 'consultant' when in reality he's a job-hopper. When he's starting work on a new project, he can forget

about how much he's missing Mum, but before long, he begins to brood. Sometimes I can tell it's happening even before he knows it himself, and I've learned to pack my bags with record speed.

I miss Mum, too.

"Well, what do you think about it, Casey?" Dad asked.

"Great!" I said, not so much because I really wanted to move again, but because I felt that Dad needed it. I know he feels guilty about disrupting my life, but in a way I don't mind the constant moving – I've never stayed in any one place for long enough to put down roots.

So, a week later, after Grandma and Grandpa had gone back home, I sat quietly in my classroom and listened to my teacher's farewell speech. My classmates seemed totally unmoved by the fact that they were going to lose me, and I felt pretty unmoved, too – I'd listened to ten other such speeches in the last four years. After I said my goodbyes, Dad and I set off on the long trip in the car filled with our belongings.

I wasn't awake when we drove into Halls. In fact, I didn't open my eyes until late the following morning, when I woke up fully

dressed, in a strange bed in a strange room. Dad must have carried me inside, because I had no memory of having made the journey myself.

My new bedroom was airy and light, with a high ceiling and white-painted walls. There was one large window with thick, dark curtains, but they were drawn back and bright sunlight was pouring in. I lifted my arm to check my watch, then let it flop back onto the bed.

It was 11:45, nearly lunchtime. I moved my head to a cooler spot on the pillow, telling myself that I'd get up before morning became afternoon. I closed my eyes for what seemed like a few seconds, preparing to face the world, then rolled out of bed and looked at my watch again. 12:25 – the few seconds had suddenly become forty minutes.

I wandered from the bedroom into the kitchen, stretching and yawning. On the table was a note from Dad, along with some lunch money.

Dear Casey,

You looked as if you were going to sleep until lunchtime, and I've had to report for work.

I've spoken to Hal, the caretaker. He's in the flat downstairs, and you can see him if you have any problems.

Call me on 555–6855 if you need me, and I'll be there in ten minutes. Spend the rest of the day unpacking and relaxing – school starts tomorrow, so enjoy your freedom! I'll be home in time to take you out for a celebration dinner.

Love, Dad.

P.S. Halls is a safe place – you can explore it, but don't go _too_ far!!!

Everything we owned was still packed in boxes, so I opened a cabinet in the kitchen, hoping to find a cup or glass to get a drink. It was empty, except for a plastic mug pushed to the back of the top shelf. The mug was one of those cheap things tourists buy, showing a fisherman with a hopeful look on his face. When I tipped the mug upside-down, a giant shark suddenly jumped out of the ocean and swallowed the unlucky angler. 'I caught a whopper at Port Maxwell' read the caption around the edge. Port Maxwell is a resort on the coast, about a thousand miles away. I'd been there once with Grandma and Grandpa, but I hadn't caught any sharks.

I rinsed the mug and had a drink. The local water tasted strange, but I knew I'd get used to it, just as I had in my last ten moves – and as I undoubtedly would in the next ten.

You can see what my life was like: in Halls for less than twelve hours, and I was already thinking about leaving. But Casey Sutch, the gypsy, was soon to find that Halls offered quite a few reasons for staying around!

Joker in the Pack

"You must be the new tenant's boy."

Startled, I glanced around and nearly stumbled on the bottom step. Standing in a doorway was the strangest-looking man I'd ever seen. He looked as if he were off to a costume party. He had long silver hair that curled down to his shoulders, and he wore a crimson silk robe, slippers that curled up at the toes, and a silver fez studded with red glass. In the darkness of the hallway he stood as trim and tall as my dad, but when I looked more closely I saw that he was at least as old as my grandpa, if not older.

"I'm Casey Sutch," I said, annoyed at being labelled 'the new tenant's boy'.

The man smiled, and there was a friendly sparkle in his eyes. "Casey Sutch. It's a good name," he said. "I'm Hal. Hal from Halls. I'm the caretaker here, and I'm one hundred and ten years old ..."

"Don't you believe him, Casey! He's a compulsive liar!" A small woman of about fifty-five stepped out of the flat.

"Well, I exaggerate," Hal admitted. "I'm really one hundred and nine. This is my wife, Barbara."

"Nice to meet you," I said.

"It's nice to meet you, too, Casey," she said. "Your father told us about you."

"Yes, he left me a note," I said.

Hal held out his hand in greeting. I shook it a little mistrustfully, half expecting a trick like a joke electric buzzer, but the shake was shock-free. Hal's grip was strong and firm, and from his long, fine fingers I wondered if he might once have been a musician.

"We've just taken a cake out of the oven. Would you care to come in and join us for a slice?" Barbara asked.

Since I had nothing better to do, I agreed. Dad's note convinced me that I could trust them. Besides, cake sounded good.

Soon we were drinking rich hot chocolate and eating meltingly soft sponge cake, in a

warm-smelling kitchen that was hardly like a kitchen at all – there was barely room for the sink. Three walls were almost covered with shelves of books and papers, propped up in rows or held down in stacks by jars of preserved fruits and vegetables. The fourth wall was made of glass, and overlooked the most fertile garden I'd ever seen.

"Green thumbs," Hal said. "Gardening's my hobby. That, plus delving into the lives of my neighbours." He laughed, and removed his fez to rub at his bald skull. Unlike his face, which was as smooth as mine, Hal's scalp was wrinkled, and it looked as if it had been pulled on in a hurry. "My books, my garden, and my tenants – three of the four corners of my existence. And Barbara's the fourth, the most important corner," he said, taking her hand and smiling.

She slapped his hand playfully. "You terrible man! Now, tell us about yourself and your father, Casey," she said.

"There's not much to tell. We're very normal," I said.

"I've never met a normal person yet," said Hal, "and I'm ..."

"... one hundred and ten," I said, finishing his sentence as I was expected to. "Tell me

about the people who lived in the flat before us."

"Before you start on another of your tales, you could offer Casey another drink," Barbara suggested. Hal obediently refilled the cups and indicated the cake plate. I didn't need a second invitation.

"Person, not people, the previous," Hal said, as I cut myself another slice of cake. "Something of a mystery, our John Holmes. Claimed to be an ornithologist, studying the local waterbirds."

"Claimed?" I asked.

"For an ornithologist, he didn't seem to know much about our feathered friends. Still, I had no real reason to doubt him."

I nodded.

"He was always coming and going, our ornithologist. Only the last time he went away, he didn't come back." Hal spoke in a light voice, but something in his tone conveyed an air of great mystery. Maybe, I decided, he'd been an actor rather than a musician.

"Go on," I requested, guiding another big chunk of cake to my mouth.

"At first I didn't do anything. He'd paid his rent in advance, and I thought that he was just off on another of his 'field trips'. But this time, weeks passed with no sign of him. Eventually I decided that I should check his flat to see whether there was anything wrong. The flat was empty, totally empty – it was as if John Holmes had never lived there. No bird-books under the bed, or hairs in the sink, or coins down the side of an armchair."

I thought of the fisherman mug I'd found. "Did you go to the police?"

"He'd probably just moved on, Casey," Hal said. He settled back in his chair and put

his hands beneath his chin, studying my face. Hal's eyes were the most unusual green I'd ever seen. They were young and full of fire, but sort of reassuring at the same time.

"Maybe he was just passing through. Travellers don't always carry very much of themselves around," I suggested. Dad and I were travellers, so I felt I could speak with some authority.

"Maybe, Casey," Hal agreed, and changed the subject. It seemed that the topic of John Holmes was closed.

Hal was a good story-spinner, but finally I managed to drag myself away, saying I should go and explore Halls before it got too late. Hal and Barbara sent me off with the left-over cake, a bag of vegetables from the garden, and a map of the town. Upstairs, I wrote a note for Dad, telling him where I was going and when I'd be back. I threw a couple of Hal's carrots and the map into my pack.

As my hand rested on the door handle, I glanced back into the flat, wondering about the fate of the missing John Holmes. I decided that Hal, a born story-teller with nothing much to do, enjoyed gathering gossip and weaving it into interesting webs. The previous tenant was probably as normal as I was. It was only in Hal's imagination that the story became fantastic.

Still, there was something about 'the John Holmes mystery' that interested me. Maybe I could investigate his disappearance. It would give me an excuse to visit Hal and Barbara – not that I'd need one. More likely, I'd need one for not dropping in.

I laughed at the thought of playing detective, and ran downstairs.

Backpacking

A sign in the main street of Halls told me that my new town had a population of two thousand. Now, with the addition of the Sutches, there were two thousand and two.

I wandered through the town centre and out along the river road, past three churches, a recreation complex, and several small factories, which I guessed were connected to the Halls Corporation.

On the outskirts of town I passed the local school – an old two-storey brick building. On the football field, a sports teacher was making her class do some kind of strange exercise routine with flags. The kids looked really odd, waving their arms and jumping around, their little flags fluttering in unison. Tomorrow, I thought, I'd be with them, waving my arms and looking just as stupid, too.

The teacher was tall and straight, and had brown hair that came halfway to her waist, so I wasn't surprised to find myself thinking of my mother; her hair had been long, too. I can remember sitting in her lap when I was little, playing with her hair while she told me stories. Like my new friend, Hal, Mum loved telling stories. Maybe, if she were still alive, they would have become friends.

There was something about the teacher that reminded me of someone else, too, but I just couldn't think who. I started to jog, excited at the chance to explore, and soon left the school far behind. As I pounded the pavement, I caught glimpses of Halls River through the trees lining its bank. Munching a carrot, I clambered over the wire fence beside the road and made my way down to the water, thinking how great it was to be enjoying the sunshine while the rest of the world was hard at work.

Halls River was about twenty metres wide, and although flowing gently, it looked deep. I pulled off my sneakers and socks and left them by my pack while I paddled my feet in

the freezing water. Then I started walking along the river-bank, looking for possible fishing spots. The grass was soft underfoot. Across the river, I could see several dull-coloured concrete buildings through the trees, with a tower like a wheat silo rising behind them. A forbidding electric fence mounted with security cameras surrounded the huge complex. Large warning signs every few metres threatened, 'Halls Corporation. Keep Out!'

So *that* was where Dad worked. Whatever he and the other scientists were working on in there, it was clear that the Corporation didn't want visitors.

I shivered, not from the cold, but from the thought of all that secret activity. I moved on, imagining that I was a spy on a top-secret mission, staying low to the ground, watchful and ready for attack. In front of me was a thick tangle of blackberry bushes, growing almost to the water-line. There was just a strip of mud between the thorns and the river. I stepped out onto the mud, sliding along the surface like an ice-skater, then slipped and almost overbalanced. I grabbed at the thorny bushes to steady myself, and to my surprise the front of a bush came away in my hands.

I stared at it. The blackberry stems had been threaded into a mesh of chicken wire to make a kind of door. Behind the 'door' was a tunnel into the thicket. Guessing that the trail led to someone's secret hide-out, I dropped to my knees and made my way in, repositioning the door behind me.

After a couple of uncomfortable minutes crawling, I reached a hollowed-out area where

I could stand up. With the light dappling through, it felt like a secret, magical world.

Glancing at my watch, I realized with a shock that it was getting late. I should get back to the flat soon, and finish exploring the hide-out on another day. I was about to crawl out again, when I noticed a flash of colour in the blackberry bushes to my left. The thing, whatever it was, was partially camouflaged under green canvas. Curious, I squeezed through the bushes and peeled back a corner, revealing a small rowing boat. Without thinking, I slipped under the canvas and sat in the boat, blinking as my eyes became accustomed to the gloom.

It was then that I saw the body, lying doubled over in the bow of the boat. Panic-stricken, I struggled to escape the suffocating folds of canvas. I scrambled out of the boat and crouched there gasping with fear. Only then did my brain register that the 'body' was not a body at all. It was a wetsuit.

Great secret agent I'd turned out to be! A wetsuit! I made myself climb back into the

boat. I knew I was being a busybody, but I wasn't doing any harm. I'd leave everything as I found it.

I began to uncover the boat's secrets. Apart from the wetsuit and two life-jackets, there was a bag of black clothing – a disguise? There were other things, too: a powerful torch; a radio scanner; some high-tech night vision glasses; and even a collapsible pick and shovel. The equipment was expensive, obviously out of a kid's price range. It looked as if the boat's owner was doing a spot of night-time digging. But why? Was he or she planning to row across the river and dig a secret tunnel under the Halls Corporation's security fence? Whatever the purpose, it was probably illegal.

Then I unearthed the last items: a thermos, and a mug showing an unlucky fisherman who'd come to a bad end at Port Maxwell – a twin to the mug I'd discovered in my flat. John Holmes' mug!

I felt sick with nerves. I should go home and speak to Dad, because he'd know what to do. Quickly I replaced the canvas, trying to make it look as if the boat hadn't been disturbed. I was about to crawl out through the tunnel of blackberries when I heard a

noise on the river. An engine! Some sort of motor boat was patrolling the river.

I thought I could hear voices over the noise, voices shouting. I doubted that anyone would spot my hiding place, but I desperately wanted to get back to my shoes and bag. Realizing that the people in the boat would probably see me if I used the tunnel, I pulled myself through the bushes, the sharp thorns tugging at my clothes and scratching my face and hands.

From a vantage point behind a large tree, I watched as a low dinghy with an outboard engine nudged around a bend in the river. The three people aboard had long poles and could have been anglers out for a little fishing, except for the fact that they were all wearing green, military-style uniforms. Security guards, I guessed.

Eventually, the dinghy slid out of sight and the engine noise receded. I waited for a few minutes before sprinting back to where I'd left my pack. Then, as I was pulling on my shoes, someone grabbed me from behind. I struggled, but the grip that held me was unbreakable.

I was trapped!

Trapped!

The restraining hands pinched into my flesh. "Turn around slowly," a voice ordered.

I did as I was told, and turned to face a tall, red-headed woman wearing a uniform similar to the one worn by the men on the boat. A large red shield on her shirt read 'Halls Corporation', and a badge identified her as J. Cross, Security Officer. "What are you doing here?" she demanded.

"Nothing. Just looking for a fishing spot. When I heard you coming I got scared and hid," I said, trying to sound innocent. It was the truth, but something about her made me feel guilty.

"This is private property."

"I didn't know that I was trespassing. I'm new in town."

"Name?"

I told her, and explained that my father had just started work with the Halls Corporation. Speaking into her radio, she asked someone in her office to confirm my story. Then she warned me to stay away from company property in the future, adding that there were some good fishing spots closer to town.

I nodded, shouldered my pack, and jogged off, relieved to have escaped. I hadn't told her about the boat. Maybe I would have if she hadn't scared the life out of me. It's hard to trust someone who's giving you a rough time,

even if she's only doing her job. I just hoped that Dad wouldn't get into trouble because of me.

I'd recovered when he got home.

"How was your day, Case?"

"Interesting," I said. "And yours?"

"Ditto," Dad said, and laughed. I could tell that he hadn't heard anything about my adventures. If he had, he would have questioned me. Maybe Security Officer J. Cross figured that she'd already done the job of scaring me off, without needing to take further action. She'd certainly scared me!

"Did you meet Hal and Barbara?" Dad asked.

"I had a snack with them. I didn't think you'd mind."

"No, they were part of the reason I chose this place to live."

"I like them," I said.

"Good."

I got the feeling that he was about to say something else about them, but instead he ushered me out the door. "Let's go find somewhere to eat. I'm hungry enough to eat a Diplodocus."

We eat out practically all the time, although Dad's actually a very good cook.

When Mum was alive, they always shared everything, the mathematical and scientific work as well as the cooking. I remember it was always fun. Maybe that's why Dad never cooks any more – he associates it with Mum.

We ate at an Italian restaurant, The Venice, and practically had the place to ourselves. The food was great, and while we ate Dad told me a little about his new job. It involved

calculations that would help to determine whether human settlements could be built on other planets.

"It's a real challenge, Casey. The Halls Corporation leads the whole world in space research, and E. Henry Halls is prepared to keep putting money into the project until we get it right."

"Isn't he the crazy boss? Have you seen him yet?"

"He wasn't there today. And I don't know that you should call him crazy, Casey; I get the feeling that he likes to work a little differently, that's all."

As we wandered back home, Dad seemed excited and sad at the same time. I knew he was thinking about his job, and that until he solved the problem he'd been hired to work on at Halls, he might sometimes seem distant. I didn't mind. That's just Dad.

As we crossed Halls Bridge, he suddenly stopped and leaned over the rail, staring into the black water. "Joy would have loved tonight," he said.

I nearly fell into the river. Dad never talked about my mother, and I'd learned not to ask. The fact that he mentioned her was amazing. Perhaps he was finally beginning to

get over her death. Four years is a long time to miss someone.

He put his arm around me. "I'm sorry I'm not the world's greatest father, Casey. I do mean to be better."

"You're not a bad dad, Dad," I said, and we both laughed.

That conversation was probably the most important I'd ever shared with Dad. And because of it, I didn't get around to telling him about my day. I didn't *mean* not to tell him about the boat, and my being caught red-handed trespassing and everything, but the opportunity passed. Then when we got home, I didn't know how to bring up the subject. Anyway, I thought, I was just some new kid who'd made a mistake; there was no need to make a big deal about it.

As I lay in bed that night, I decided that there was a perfectly normal explanation for the boat being in the blackberry bushes. John Holmes had told Hal that he was an ornithologist. If he'd been studying birds on the river, it would explain the boat and the binoculars, and maybe even the wetsuit. Some ornithologists might want to study their subjects from the water.

I should never have listened to Hal with all his hints of mysteries – really there was nothing mysterious at all. And Dad had enough to think about without listening to my silly fantasies.

I went to sleep and dreamt of flags, hot chocolate, and black rubber wetsuits.

CHAPTER 5

Cross Words

"You're the boy they caught by the river."

I stopped and turned to look at the girl who'd approached me as I crossed the school playground, wondering how she knew.

"This is a small town. Everyone knows absolutely everything," she said, laughing at my expression. She had a nice face.

"Oh!" I said, feeling like the only person in Halls who didn't know everything.

"My mother was the guard who caught you," she explained.

"That was your mother! I've still got big bruises where she grabbed me," I said jokingly.

"She has a black belt in karate."

"I believe you," I said, rubbing my arm.

The girl laughed again. Like her mother, she had red hair, and seemed as if she could take care of herself.

"I'd better go and enrol," I said. "I don't want to start off on the wrong foot."

"You already have, by trespassing on the company's property," the karate expert's daughter said.

I shrugged.

"I'll take you to the office, if you like. I'm Caroline Cross."

I told her my name, and because she seemed genuinely friendly, I accepted her offer. We started walking towards the school building. I got a few interested looks from the other students, but they soon forgot about me and went back to their games.

"Where have you come from, Casey?" Caroline asked as we walked down some steps.

"I'd need practically all the time in the world to tell you that."

"Yeah?" Caroline asked, interested.

"My dad and I have moved a lot," I explained.

"I've always lived in Halls," Caroline said. "It's pretty good here, but sometimes I think I wouldn't mind going somewhere else."

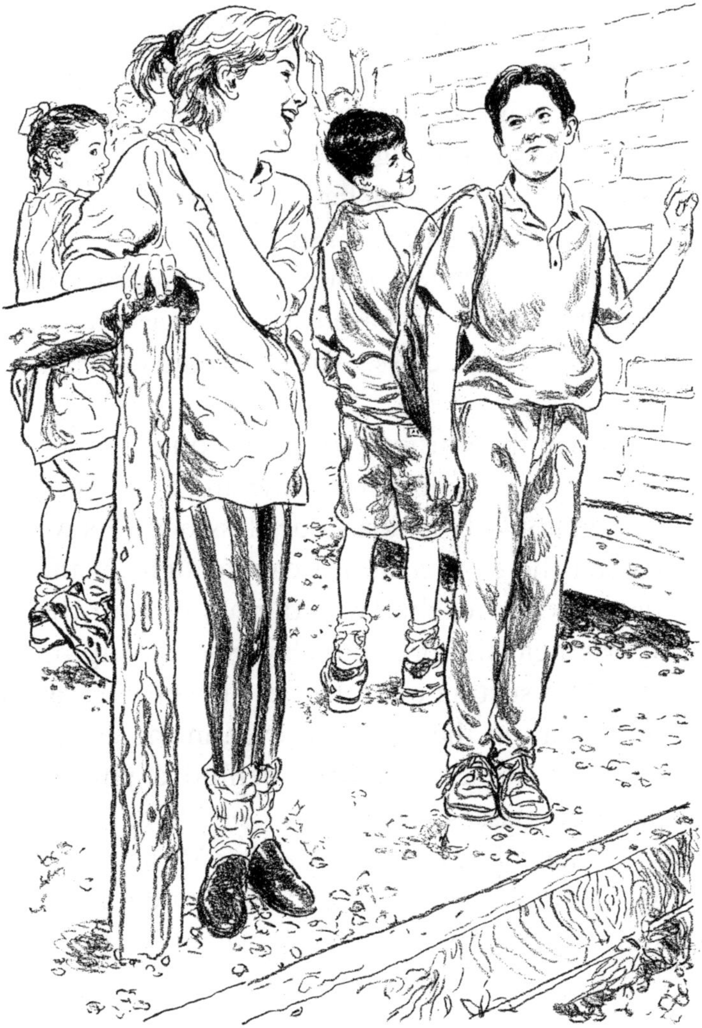

"I wouldn't mind staying put for once," I said. "This is my eleventh school since my mother died four years ago." I stopped, astonished to have heard the words coming from my mouth. Normally I keep to myself when I start a new school, yet here I was telling personal things to a total stranger. The red hair must have had a more powerful effect on me than I realized.

Caroline waited around while I enrolled, and she seemed pleased when I was put in Mr Harrison's class. Mr Harrison was her teacher.

When the music sounded to announce the beginning of school, Caroline and I followed a crowd of kids towards our classroom. As we passed the gymnasium, I caught sight of the flag-waving teacher who'd been out on the sports field the previous day. She was up on the stage sorting out a basket of ropes. It was quite dark in the gym, but even in the gloom she had her eyes hidden behind a pair of large sunglasses.

"That's The Generator – alias Ms Jennings. Watch out for her," Caroline warned as we walked on. "She might look like a china doll, but she's as tough as, um …"

"Nails?" I suggested.

"... my mother's roast beef," said Caroline, with a grin. "The Generator only started here this year, but boy, has she made her mark! She's absolutely crazy about exercises with flags. Has us doing them in almost every lesson. Sometimes we'll be in the middle of something else, like basketball, and suddenly she'll make us stop what we're doing, and out come the flags. It's really weird."

That would help to explain the crazy semaphoring I'd seen the day before. "Maybe she owns a flag factory," I said.

Caroline laughed; then her voice dropped to a conspiratorial whisper. "I think she's a spy."

"Yeah?" I said, uneasy at the use of the word 'spy'. After the discovery of the boat in the blackberries, and Hal's story of John Holmes' disappearance, even a tall story about a schoolteacher spy seemed possible. Perhaps in a town like Halls, home to a top-secret research facility, people were *always* thinking of spies and espionage.

"No, really!" said Caroline. "I think she's stealing inventions and things from the Halls plant, and then she's using us to signal her secrets. All that flag-waving is some kind of code. I hear lots of things about the Corporation from my mum," she added mysteriously.

"That's ridiculous," I said, but I felt a shiver run up my spine.

"It's not ridiculous," Caroline insisted. "She could be sending messages to an enemy satellite. A satellite could have special sensors to pick up the signals."

"There'd be simpler ways of doing it," I said.

"Name one!" Caroline demanded angrily.

"Putting the information in the mail, or using carrier pigeons," I said, trying to lighten the situation. "That's two ways."

"And you're just a pigeon-brain," Caroline snapped back. "You've only been here for a day, and you think you know everything."

"How could she even get in there to spy? The place is like a fortress."

"For your information, Mr Smartypants, she could easily get in because she's the company's fitness co-ordinator. She runs programmes for the staff. So, stick that up your jumper and I hope it keeps you warm on winter nights. We're here."

She pushed past me to her desk. I stood at the front, waiting for Mr Harrison and wishing that I'd agreed with everything Caroline had said. Stupid me – I'd lost my chance of an easy entry into my new school. Still, how could she have expected me to believe her stupid story? She'd probably just been trying to impress me, or to see whether I was just a gullible new kid who'd believe anything.

School began. I was introduced to the class, and then I got stuck into work, not wanting Mr Harrison to think I was a dunce. I'm not. I like learning.

Caroline ignored me. In one way I didn't mind, because I'm always a bit of a loner at school. In another way, I did mind. I liked Caroline Cross. But since there's absolutely no use crying over spilt lemonade, I put my head down and got on with my maths assignment. So began my career at school number eleven.

CHAPTER 6

Crossed Flags

I soon settled into my new school. After a few days of giving me the icy shoulder, Caroline forgave me. Although I still didn't buy her story about Ms Jennings being an industrial spy, she was right about one thing: The Generator was obsessed with waving flags. I discovered this after accidentally dropping a flag during my first lesson with her. Ms Jennings didn't blow her stack, but she lowered her voice to a whisper that made my blood run cold. I decided to be very careful around her in the future.

There was something about Ms Jennings that puzzled me, too. Her voice, and the way she stood, seemed familiar, but I couldn't think why. And in my first week at school, I'd never once seen her without her sunglasses.

Still, I thought as I walked home at the end of the day, none of these things made Ms Jennings a spy. I started thinking about Hal and Barbara, instead. It had already become a habit for me to drop in to their place when I got home. We'd drink hot chocolate and chat about this and that. I think that they genuinely liked my company, and I was a bit flattered by the attention. I found myself telling them far more about the Sutches than I'd normally tell anyone.

Yet as much as I liked Hal, there was something different about him. Sometimes I felt there was something strange going on behind those unusual green eyes, but at the same time I couldn't imagine that there was any more to him than he claimed – he was just someone with green thumbs and a taste for cake and stories.

After the episode by the river with Caroline's mother, I decided I wasn't cut out to be a detective. I deliberately didn't pursue my 'inquiries' into the disappearance of John Holmes – the only mysteries I wanted were in the detective stories I borrowed from the school library.

And so, steadily, my life in Halls settled into a routine. That is, until one Thursday afternoon – I'd been downstairs to visit Hal and Barbara, but strangely, they weren't home. I was halfway up the hallway, when I heard the sound of a key in a lock. Turning, I saw Ms Jennings letting herself into Hal and Barbara's flat.

Ms Jennings!

What was she doing going into their place? I asked myself. What was she doing letting herself in? She couldn't even *know* Hal and Barbara. But it was her, definitely: the sunglasses and the long thick hair that looked almost unreal.

What was going on? I found my head spinning with crazy thoughts. Where were my neighbours? They were usually at home when I called. I thought of Ms Jennings, and her sunglasses, and the fact that she reminded me of someone I knew. Who was it? It had been nagging at me since my first day in Halls. My mother? Yes, but there was something else. It was a man. Hal? It was Hal! They were the same height; had the same way of standing very upright; had similar noses.

The weirdest thought struck me. Perhaps Ms Jennings and Hal were one and the same person, playing different roles in order to do something illegal at the Halls plant. So Barbara must be part of the plot, too. Maybe she helped with the wigs and make-up and things.

No, it was ridiculous. I was imagining crazy things, and it was all Caroline's fault for starting her nonsense about spies.

But at the same time, it seemed crazy enough to be true! Perhaps Hal wasn't just the caretaker he claimed he was, but a master (or mistress!) of disguises – acting as Ms Jennings some of the time in order to steal secrets from the Halls Corporation. After all, I only had Hal's word for it that John Holmes existed; maybe the boat that I'd found belonged to Hal/Ms Jennings.

For a moment I really thought hard about confronting The Generator in Hal and Barbara's flat, but I didn't have the nerve.

Her cold whisper would have scared off a heavyweight boxer. I tiptoed on and ran up the stairs, telling myself over and over that I was being really stupid. Hal couldn't be Ms Jennings. They were complete opposites: old, young; male, female; gentle, ferocious!

He couldn't be!

Could he?

For the rest of the afternoon, I kept one eye on the front window, watching and waiting. I didn't see Hal or Barbara returning, and I didn't see Ms Jennings leave. But she was at school the next morning.

It was then that I made a decision. At the first opportunity, I'd unmask her. Somehow I'd get to see her eyes behind her sunglasses. Without the glasses, she'd find it hard to disguise the extraordinary eyes of the man I knew as Hal.

The next day, I followed Ms Jennings everywhere. Wherever she went, I shadowed her. I followed her from the assembly hall to the staffroom, and from the staffroom to the basketball courts, hoping she'd remove her sunglasses so that I could see her eyes. But not once did she even look as though she was going to take them off, and this fact only made me all the more convinced that she was hiding something. A normal person doesn't wear sunglasses twenty-four hours a day.

I wasted my whole lunchbreak because Ms Jennings spotted me tailing her and sent me off to pack up some equipment in the gym. When Caroline came in and asked me what I'd done to deserve hard labour, I told her I was doing it because I enjoyed it. She went off in a huff.

My class had a physical education lesson that afternoon, and sure enough, the first activity was flags. It was as boring as ever, but everyone tried really hard. If we didn't get it right, Ms Jennings would make us do it again and again, and we'd never be allowed to do anything more interesting.

"Okay, class – you're getting there, but let's try that routine once again. Everyone try to follow Samantha. One, two, three," Ms Jennings directed.

I moved closer to Ms Jennings, my flags twirling. She was nodding her head, a small smile on her face, because our co-ordination was almost perfect.

Closer, closer.

"Left flag, then right flag," Ms Jennings ordered. "Left flag ..."

Now!

I straggled out of line, my flags still moving, hoping to get close enough to her to see behind her sunglasses.

Ms Jennings noticed me getting closer and turned around sharply to glare.

"... right flag."

Instinctively I thrust out my right arm, and – crack! – hit her under the chin with my flag. I didn't mean to, of course; it was a dreadful accident.

Down went Ms Jennings like a house of cards. A shock wave passed around the class. Brian Hunt, on my left, stepped away, not wanting to be too close to me when she woke up.

54

Caroline dropped her flags and crouched beside Ms Jennings, feeling for a pulse. "You're lucky, Casey Sutch, she's still alive. You won't have to face a murder charge."

I let out a relieved breath. Ms Jennings had hit the ground so hard that it looked as if I might have killed her. Suddenly, she started to move, and Caroline helped her to sit up. Ms Jennings shook her head, obviously confused.

"It's all right, Ms Jennings," Caroline reassured her. "Casey Sutch just knocked you unconscious."

Thanks a lot, pal, I thought.

"I always knew that teaching was a dangerous profession," Ms Jennings said, and to my surprise, she started laughing. Maybe the blow had knocked her senseless.

Fortunately she wasn't seriously injured, and the lesson resumed. I picked up my flags and followed the routine, unhappy because I'd failed in my objective – I hadn't succeeded in seeing her eyes, so I hadn't discovered if Ms Jennings was really Hal.

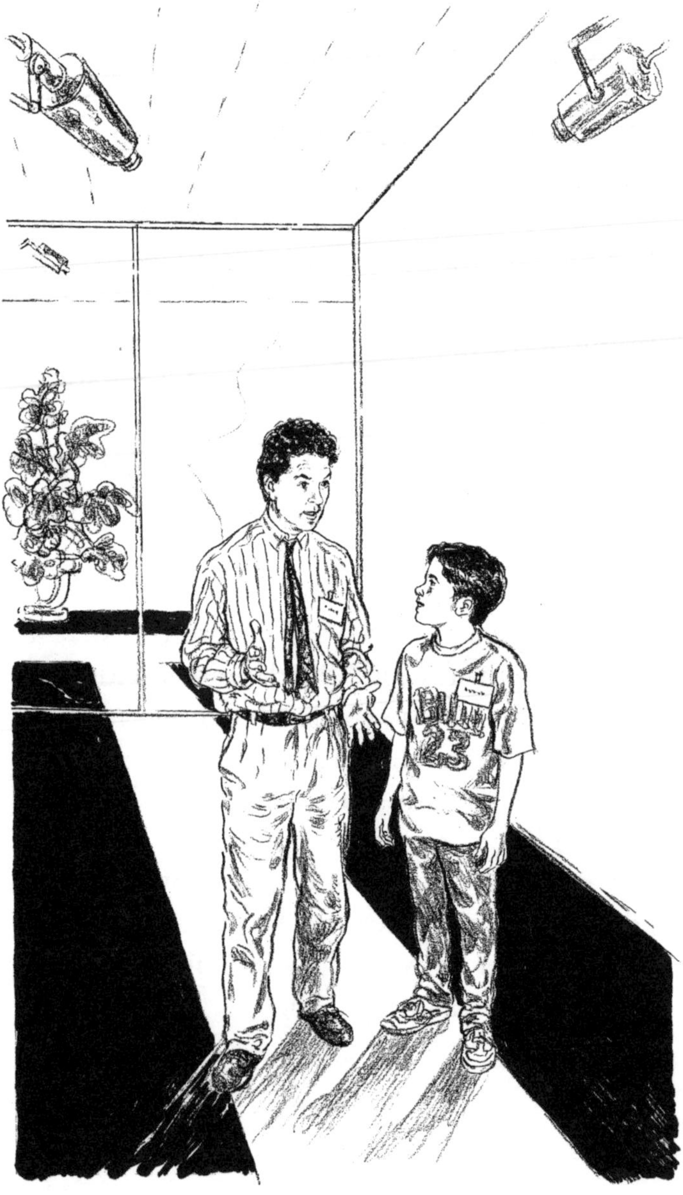
23

CHAPTER 7

Crossed Wires?

Not long after I'd almost brained Ms Jennings, Dad was given permission to show me around the Halls complex. So, one Saturday morning, I clipped on my green visitor's pass and went for my first proper look inside the security fence. It was great, especially getting to see Boris, the mainframe computer. There were secret areas where I couldn't go, but that didn't stop me imagining what went on behind the locked doors.

"Still want to be a scientist when you grow up, Case?" Dad asked. I nodded happily. Seeing where Dad worked had helped to take my mind off my worries about Hal.

We were on our way out when a balding, middle-aged man materialized from a big office. A sign on the door read: 'Dr Roger Roberts, Head of Research'.

"So you're the genius's son," he said, when Dad had introduced me. From the way he spoke, it was obvious that he didn't like children. I got the sense that he didn't like Dad much, either.

I nodded, but Dr Roberts had started talking to Dad as if they were the only ones in the place. It seemed that he didn't agree with something Dad had written in a report, and he was trying to convince Dad he was wrong.

"I'm sorry, Roger, the numbers don't lie," Dad insisted, refusing to be bullied. "You're quite welcome to have someone else go over my work."

That's Dad all over. He'll do his job, even if it means treading on a few toes. For him, numbers are everything.

"Well, have it your way, Sutch. I don't think we'll be seeing you around for much longer," said Dr Roberts, and stomped back into his office.

"Sorry about that, Casey," said Dad.

"I wasn't worried," I said, half-truthfully.

There was something strange about Dr Roberts's aggressive attitude to my father.

"Let's go fishing. I have the gear in the car," Dad suggested.

"Okay, great," I said.

We headed out, arm in arm.

Dad, I hate to confess, is not a good fisherman. Something about standing by a river makes his mind go into overdrive. You can almost hear the gears shifting as he thinks his own thoughts rather than concentrating on the fish. He doesn't believe me when I say that the game between an angler and a trout is like a game of chess.

After a couple of hours (during which Dad caught and released two brown trout and I caught ... nothing) we went home, stopping on the way to pick up a pizza for a late lunch. We sat in the kitchen of our apartment eating pizza with our fingers, and reading out jokes from my *Chunky* magazine. Dad has the same offbeat sense of humour as me, but he hasn't laughed much for ages. When Mum was alive, we used to joke all the time. I remember her laugh – it's one of my favourite memories of her.

"Okay, here's a good one. There was a woman with twelve children living in …" The phone rang. Dad put down the magazine and went to answer it.

"That was the President of Halls on the phone, Casey," Dad said when he came back. "He wants to see me."

"Why? Is there something going on, Dad?"

"It's okay, Case, he only wants to discuss my project."

There was something strange about his tone. "But it's Saturday. Are you in trouble, Dad? Is it to do with what Dr Roberts was talking about today?"

"Everything's fine. I'll tell you about it later. Or do you want to come with me?"

"No thanks. I'd better do my homework." For some reason, I didn't believe Dad's reassurance, and I didn't want to be in the way if he had a difficult meeting on his hands. I felt in my bones that it had something to do with Dr Roberts, and that if *he* had his way, Dad was going to be dismissed. It looked like it might be bag-packing time again for the Sutches, even sooner than usual.

"I don't know how long I'll be," he said. "If you need anything, go and see Hal." He looked at me strangely. "On second thoughts, ring me on my work number. I'll be in the conference room."

"Okay, Dad."

He found his car keys and left. Why had he changed his mind about telling me to contact Hal? I knew it was crazy, but I'd been avoiding Hal and Barbara ever since I'd seen Ms Jennings going into their apartment. Now it looked as if Dad was beginning to have his suspicions about Hal, too.

Our place seemed incredibly empty without Dad. I cleared away the pizza mess and got out my homework, a project about the history of money. About fifteen minutes later, the phone rang. Without taking my eyes off my book, I reached for the handset.

There was a scrabbling sound and the noise of breathing, and then a muffled voice spoke. "I'm warning you not to go to that meeting, Sutch," it threatened. "You and your brat should get out of town before there's trouble."

Before I could respond, there was a sharp click as the caller hung up.

I sat there in shock, my thoughts a complete jumble. Someone was after Dad. Perhaps the person who'd spoken to him was only pretending to be the President of Halls, and the meeting he'd gone to was a trap. And the second caller, the threatening caller, had assumed that I was Dad, not knowing that he'd already left for the plant.

So who was the first caller, and who was the second? I put two and two together and it didn't add up. I needed Sherlock Holmes to help me find the answers to my questions, but he was unavailable. I was going to have to do this on my own.

It had to be a trap!

I pulled on my sneakers and jumper, ran downstairs, and banged on Hal's door. This was no time for suspicion – I needed his help. "Come on, come on!"

No response. So where was Hal? Was he really mixed up in this after all?

I kicked the door in fury, and ran out into the street, heading for the boat in the blackberries. I didn't think about what I was doing; I just did it. My father was in danger.

CHAPTER 8

Crossing the Line

I pulled the boat through the tunnel of thorns, ignoring the scratches. Holding the bowline, I dragged it to the river's edge. The noise of the water slapping at the boards of the rowing boat sounded as loud as gunshots in the stillness.

I jumped in, pulled out one of the lifejackets, and put my foot over the side, ready to push off. The boat rocked wildly, and I nearly tumbled into the river. I steadied myself and the boat. I had to rescue my father. I couldn't let myself give in to panic.

"Come on, Casey," I told myself, and took a deep breath.

Suddenly, a heavy hand grabbed me from behind. I stopped dead, my heart pounding with fear.

"What are you doing?" demanded a voice. I gasped with relief. It wasn't Halls Corporation security. But it *was* security's daughter: my classmate, Caroline Cross.

"My dad's at work. He's in danger," I gasped, my breathing slowly returning to normal.

"Do you think Ms Jennings is involved?"

"Yes! No! I don't know. Something funny's going on. I've got to get across the river to the plant. Don't hold me up."

"Get aboard," Caroline ordered.

"What are you doing?"

"Coming with you. I can get in and out of the grounds easily. I've been doing it since I could walk."

Needing all the help I could get, I accepted her offer.

Caroline got out the second life-jacket and pushed off. She jumped in and took the oars. "I saw you racing past my place and guessed something was up, and so I followed you," she said, bending her head to the oars and guiding the boat upstream in fluid, easy strokes.

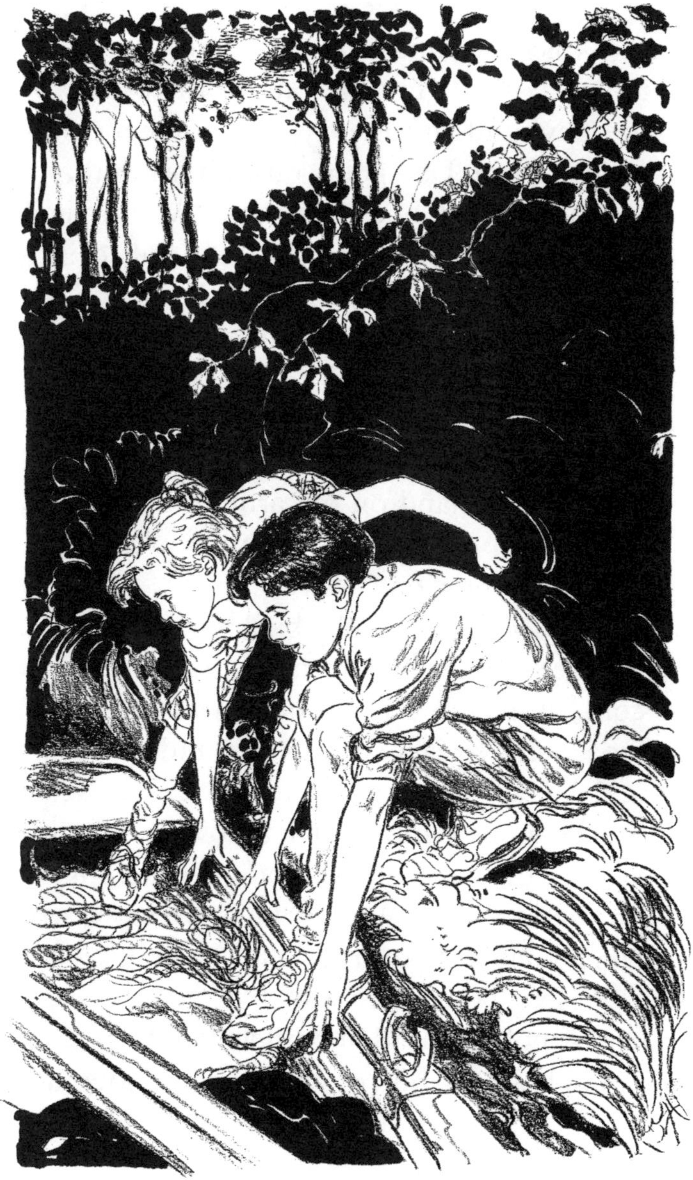

I told Caroline about the boat, and John Holmes. And I told her about the events of the day, and my theory that someone was trying to stop Dad going on with his work.

She nodded, and then said, "We can land here." A moment later the boat pulled into the opposite bank with a gentle bump. "Keep your voice down. There are cameras and things," she warned.

"I've seen them," I told her.

"Yes, and they saw you," said Caroline. She put her hand on my arm and squeezed, reminding me of my encounter with her mother. "Come on."

She led me on to the bank. It was scary in the trees. Sounds were magnified, and I felt cold all over. Even Caroline was silent and tense, and I reached for her hand. Soon we arrived at the security fence. Up close, it looked impassable, but I followed Caroline around the perimeter, keeping a watchful eye on the security cameras, until we came to a large, hollowed-out tree.

"Here," Caroline said.

I shook my head, not understanding.

"There's a burrow that goes under this tree to the other side of the fence," Caroline said triumphantly.

"An animal's burrow?" I said.

"It hasn't been used for years, except by me," Caroline said with a grin. "And don't worry. It's not going to cave in. A geologist came to school once, and said the ground around here is incredibly stable. That's why it's used for rocket experiments."

"What about spiders and things?"

"You're a big boy; if a spider jumps on you, just say *boo!*"

"Very funny."

"Come on," said Caroline, ducking into the base of the tree. "There are no creepy-crawlies." I heard her scrabbling around inside, and then she was gone. Swallowing, I followed. If she could do it, so could I. After all, it was my dad we were on the way to rescue.

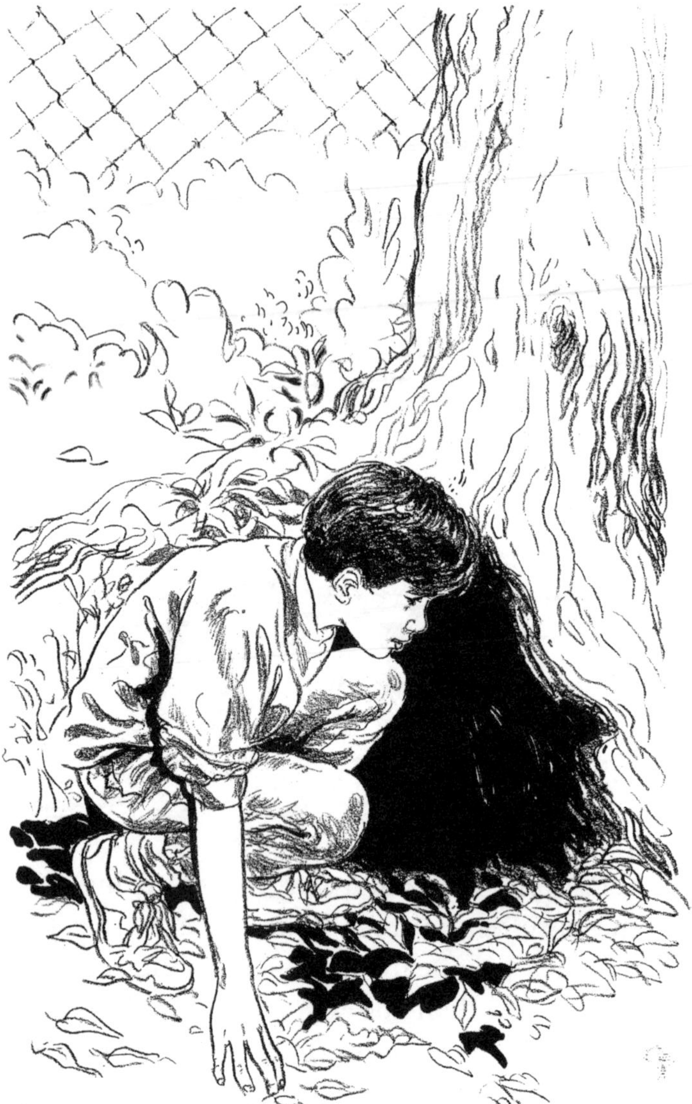

My stomach churned as I entered the darkness. I'm not very good with enclosed places. It's not that I thought the tunnel would cave in or anything, because I could see that it was well-made and solid. It's just that I've always found it hard to breathe when I'm shut in. I like light, airy places.

"C'mon, Case, you can do it," I told myself, and slid into the hole. I pulled myself along the rock floor of the dark tunnel, and tried to shut my mind to any thoughts except getting to the end and rescuing Dad.

It seemed to take forever to drag myself over a small distance, and I felt like screaming with happiness when I saw the light. I don't think I've ever felt more relieved than when Caroline reached down and pulled me out into the open.

I stood, breathing heavily and brushing myself off, half expecting some words of praise from her. But Caroline simply said, "This way," and led me through a maze of trees and bushes.

We skirted a cluster of buildings and splashed through a small creek, stopping occasionally to watch and listen before daring to move on. At last we came to the administration building and I saw Dad's car alone in the carpark. If the President had come too, he hadn't parked here. Desperately I studied the situation. The doors were computer-controlled, and it wasn't the sort of place where doors were accidentally left open. Without a plastic security pass, we were stuck on the outside.

"Can you get me in?" I asked Caroline hopefully.

Caroline shook her head. "I'm sorry."

"I have to get inside."

"Perhaps you should go to the police, Casey," Caroline said, sensing I was getting desperate.

"I have to do something before it's too late," I said. "You go home if you want to."

But Caroline didn't respond. She grabbed my arm, hushing me.

"What?" I whispered.

"Someone's coming."

I held my breath, concentrating. After a moment I heard the sound of a small engine, possibly a motorbike. It was coming towards us. Caroline pulled me down. We watched as a black-leathered motorcyclist cruised up and parked right next to the door, obviously not bothered about being observed.

The rider wore a black helmet and dark glasses, and looked far too dangerous to tackle, even though I had a karate champion's daughter for assistance. Besides, I couldn't ask Caroline to risk her life.

The motorcyclist switched off the bike and removed his helmet, letting his long hair cascade over his shoulders.

But it wasn't a he. It was Ms Jennings!

Caroline's fingers pinched into my arm. I was shaking, fear battling with rage. Ms Jennings punched what must have been a pass code into the computer.

"See, I was right," Caroline whispered, her eyes wide. "She must be a spy."

As Ms Jennings waited for the door to open, she removed her sunglasses. It was such a natural movement that for a second I didn't register that she'd actually taken them off. Then my mouth dropped open. Even from a distance, there was no mistaking it. Ms Jennings, apart from the hair, thirty years and a sex change, could have been Hal.

It looked as if *I'd* been right, too! Ms Jennings/Hal was a spy, and my father was in danger. The door opened, and Ms Jennings disappeared into the depths of the Halls Corporation.

"Come on!" I dragged Caroline to the door, and we slipped in just before it closed.

CHAPTER 9

An Open-and-shut Case

We followed Ms Jennings's footsteps through the darkened hallways until she entered the conference room. There were lights on, and I could see Dad seated with his back to the door. Ms Jennings was standing to the side, her long hair swinging, the look on her face cold and dangerous. There was a third person sitting just out of the line of my vision.

Then a door at the rear opened and Dr Roger Roberts swaggered in. The Head of Research glanced around the room before sitting down at the far end of the table. He drummed his fingers on the hard wood. To me, it sounded like the drum roll before an execution – my dad's execution!

Suddenly, I knew who the threatening caller had been. Dr Roberts! Unable to stop myself, I burst into the room, shrieking, "Let him go!" and then, "Hal ...?" Hal was the mysterious third person. But that meant he wasn't Ms Jennings!

"Casey, you're here, too. Isn't this nice," Hal said pleasantly. "We've been expecting you – the security team spotted you and this young lady on your way through the grounds. You always seem to know when a mug of hot chocolate's on offer." He indicated a tray on the conference table.

"What's going on?" I asked, turning to my father.

But it was Hal who spoke. "I think it's about time I introduced myself properly," he said. "My full name is Edward Henry Halls, and I own this company." A door opened, and Barbara came into the room, carrying an armful of files and official-looking documents. "And Barbara," Hal continued, "is Company Director, and the board member responsible for overseeing our space programme."

My head was reeling. Hal and Barbara, my cosy neighbours, were really the Halls Corporation bigwigs? What next? Then Hal continued: "This person," he said, indicating Ms Jennings, "is my niece. You, of course, know her as your teacher, but she's also been doing a bit of detective work for me. I have a niece who's a brilliant amateur detective. Isn't that what everyone would wish for?"

"No, Uncle, not really," Ms Jennings said, and smiled. Smiled! Boy, things were really proving strange today. First Hal and Barbara, now The Generator. But I was right about something. There was a resemblance between Hal and Ms Jennings – I hadn't been that far off the mark.

Hal saw the puzzled look on my face and laughed. "You know your father, of course, Casey, and I believe that you've already met Dr Roberts."

"Yes," I managed to gasp, and Dr Roberts glared at me.

Barbara took a seat at the head of the table, and asked me to introduce Caroline, while Hal offered us a drink. "Dr Roberts?" he asked, holding out a steaming mug.

The Head of Research ignored the hot chocolate, and glared at the group gathered around the table. "Is someone going to explain this tomfoolery?" he demanded.

"All in good time, Roger. Let's finish our drinks first," Barbara said lightly. So we sipped away politely, even though I was bursting to know what was going on.

When we were ready, Hal looked at Dad and said, "Well, I guess it's over to you, Jacob."

Dad stood up. "I've told you a little about what I've been working on, haven't I, Casey."

"Yes, it's to do with determining whether humans can settle on other planets."

"That's right. It's part of a project that was initiated by Dr Roberts. I think I'm right in saying that, Roger?"

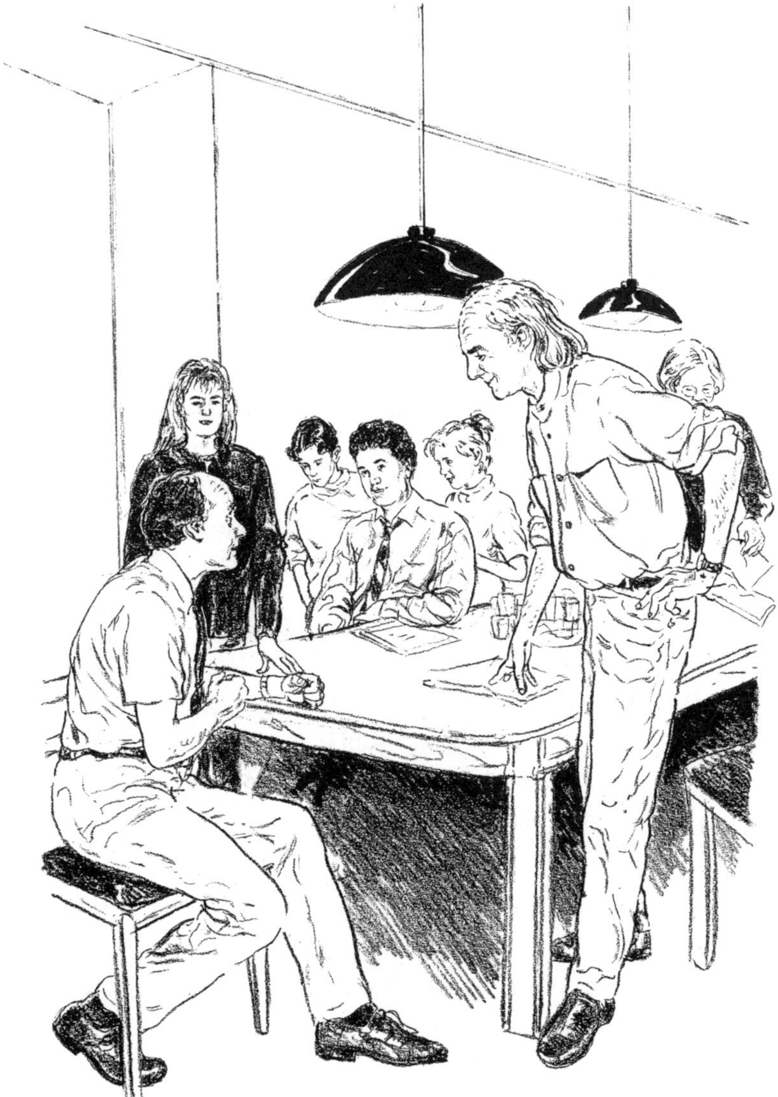

Dr Roberts shrugged.

"I was hired as a troubleshooter, to solve some problems the Corporation thought the project had run into," Dad continued.

"What problems, Sutch?" Dr Roberts said threateningly.

"Simple, Roger; the project's not going to work, because the mathematical calculations are way out."

"You're not a scientist, Sutch, you're nothing but a jumped-up number cruncher."

"Maybe, Roger, but just the same this jumped-up number cruncher has worked out how you've been cheating."

The Head of Research rose, looking as if he wanted to strangle my father.

"Sit down, Dr Roberts," Ms Jennings demanded in her quiet, dangerous voice.

He glared at her but did as he was told, just as we students did in our flag-waving lessons.

"Light that Bunsen burner, Casey," Dad said.

There was a gas burner set up on the table. I went over to it and lit the gas while Dad collected a beaker of icicles from the bar fridge. He selected one and held it up. "See this, an icicle, frozen water. What will happen if I heat it up?"

You didn't need to be a Nobel Prize winner to answer that. "The ice will turn into water and then into steam," I said.

"Right, solid to liquid to gas." Dad tapped the icicle on the side of the Bunsen burner and then held it over the flame. The ice quickly started to bubble at the edges as it vaporized. Drops of water spilt onto the burner, hissing ferociously. Dad tapped the burner again and said, "Solid." Then he waved his hand through the steam like a magician and said, "Permeable."

He repeated the process.

"Solid." He tapped.

"Permeable." He waved.

I nodded to show that I understood.

"Okay, if I wanted to, I could collect the steam, refreeze it, and make it solid again," Dad continued. "But now imagine if something could be a solid and a gas *at the same time*. If it could act as a barrier," – he knocked his palm against the tabletop – "yet also allow solid things to pass through it." He pushed his hand through the air.

He continued. "What I'm talking about is a totally sealed dome, sheltering a colony of scientists, on a planet where conditions are vastly different from those on Earth. This dome would act as an impervious barrier to the atmospheric conditions which would otherwise make it impossible for human life to exist there. At the same time, the molecular make-up of the dome's surface would allow easy access and exit points for exploratory rockets, and other vehicles. What I'm saying is that solid objects could pass right through

the apparently solid surface of the dome. This does away with the need for doors, and other structures that might make the dome more likely to collapse under the incredible atmospheric pressure of the planet."

"It sounds too weird, Dad, like something out of a science fiction movie."

"The Halls Corporation has just spent close to a hundred million dollars trying to prove that it's not impossible," Hal said. He didn't look like a man who had a hundred dollars to spend, let alone a hundred million. He continued, "At this particular time, you're right, Casey; we don't yet have the knowledge to make something solid and gaseous at the same time. We were convinced that we were coming pretty close. But whenever we got to a certain point, the experiments failed, and we couldn't work out why. In fact, it almost looked as if the whole project were being sabotaged."

Hal was looking at me, but his words were directed to Dr Roberts. The Head of Research stood up. "I'm not going to stay here, listening to this fairytale."

"Roger, you'll stay," Barbara ordered. Again Dr Roberts did as he was told, an amused smile on his face.

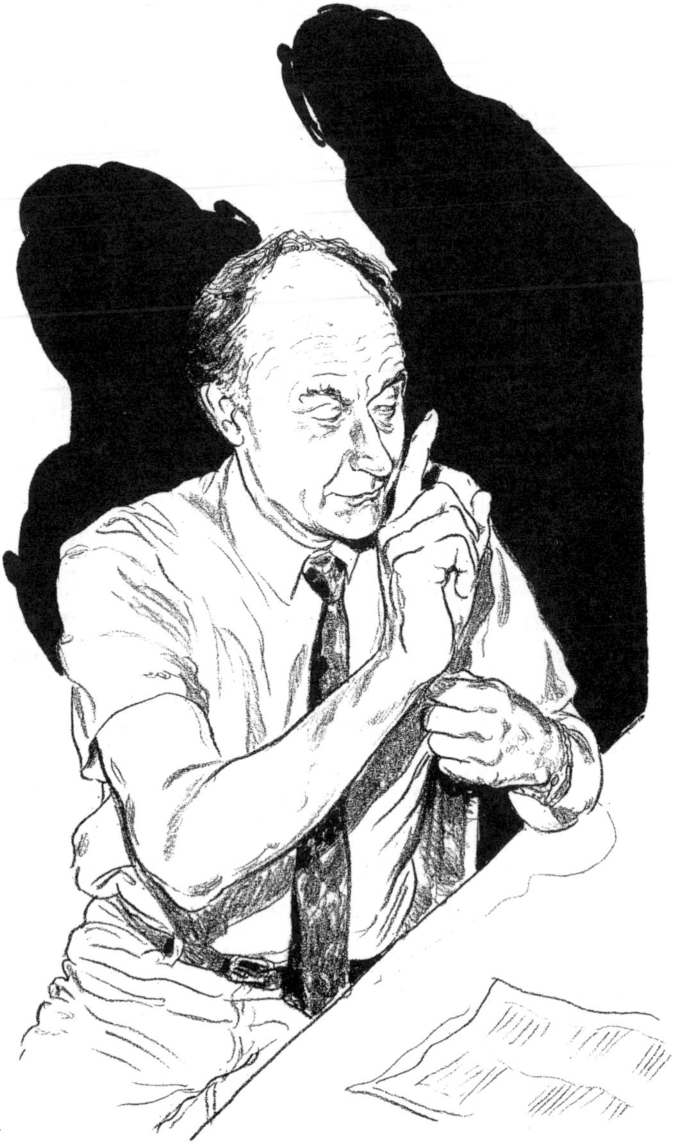

"Does John Holmes fit into this?" I asked, looking at Barbara, then Hal.

"Yes, Casey," said Barbara, "he does. He was hired by a person or persons unknown," – she looked at Dr Roberts, who sat with his head down, seemingly fascinated by the wood grain in the table top – "to steal the computer programmes which had convinced us to fund the research in the first place. This person thought that by destroying the original data and replacing it with concocted information, he or she could sabotage the entire project. However, unfortunately for the saboteur, John Holmes became greedy and decided to go after other research secrets on his own behalf, thinking that he could sell them to one of our business rivals. Luckily for Halls, our niece became suspicious and discovered what he was doing."

"Mr Holmes was sent packing, but not before he told us exactly how he came to be here in the first place," Ms Jennings added. She smiled dangerously at Dr Roberts, who was digging splinters of wood out of the table with his fingernails.

Hal spoke, his voice no longer that of my eccentric landlord, but of a powerful company director. "If John Holmes hadn't bitten off more than he could chew, we would probably never have discovered Roger's little game!"

Dr Roberts began to clap loudly. "Very clever. It's a pity you're never going to be able to prove any of this. I've just come from checking Boris, and an unfortunate power surge has erased the relevant data. And," he added triumphantly, "all of the backup data has disappeared." He smiled. "You're not going to be able to prove anything against me, and if any of you try, I'll see you in court."

"Not quite true, Roger," Dad said. "I took the precaution of copying all the data on the system on my first day. And I've been making my own backups ever since, just in case this sort of 'unfortunate accident' happened. To coin a phrase, your number's up! You've been foiled by a jumped-up number cruncher." He took a computer disk out of his pocket, and waved it with a flourish.

Dr Roberts glared at him. "I'll get you, Sutch."

"You're not getting anyone, Roger. You're going to gaol." Barbara pressed a bell and Caroline's mother stepped into the room. "Dr Roberts is leaving us, Jennifer."

Security Guard Cross escorted him out, her ferocious grip firm on his arm. Dr

Roberts's head was bent, and he'd lost the aggression he'd shown just a minute before.

Hal spoke. "It's amazing how close we were to success until Roger sold out to one of our rivals. A few calculations were all that stood between the project being feasible and its being impossible. I feel sorry for him in a way."

"Why?" Caroline asked. There'd been so much going on in the preceding ten minutes, she hadn't said a word before this.

"Dr Roger Roberts was once a brilliant researcher, and at first, he really believed in this project. Then he hit a low point. He lost his life savings when his investments failed, and he started telling himself that he was a failure in his work, too. His research had all been right on track until then, but he convinced himself that he would never get to the end. He could have stopped the project, but he felt that his scientific reputation was on the line. Then one of our rivals offered him a very large sum of money to sabotage the project.

"Roger started to fiddle with the data he and the research team had collated, throwing the calculations out. Because he was Head of Research he could cover his tracks pretty successfully, and no one else here had the mathematical expertise to figure out where things were going wrong. So that's what Roberts was doing for the last twelve months – that is, until Jacob joined Halls."

"One hundred million dollars wasted!" Caroline breathed.

"Not totally, Caroline," Barbara added. "There are always benefits to scientific research. And now, with the mathematical work Jacob has done over the past month, it seems we might yet be able to salvage the project."

"And now," said Hal, "it's getting late, and I think that you detectives should be getting home for your dinners."

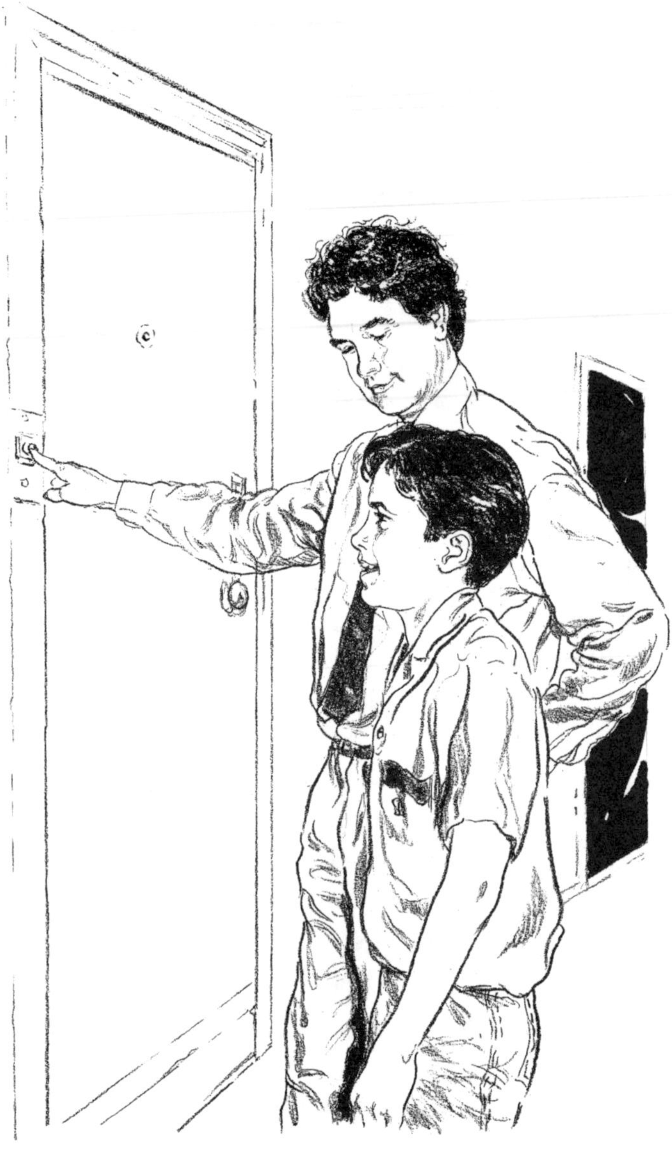

EPILOGUE

The Case Is Closed

It seemed that with Roger Roberts caught, there wasn't any reason for the Sutches to remain in Halls. The next night, Dad and I went downstairs to tell Hal and Barbara that we'd be moving out of the apartment. Before we could break our news, they insisted we sit down for hot chocolate and cake. Now that my questions about Hal had been answered, I knew I'd miss him and Barbara. Their place had become a kind of second home.

A smile passed between Dad and Hal, and I remembered something that had been bothering me since yesterday. I turned to Dad. "Why didn't you tell me at the start who Hal was?"

"I'm sorry for not being totally truthful, Casey, but I knew that if Hal and Barbara's suspicions about Dr Roberts were correct, then I could be taking you into a dangerous situation. They and I both thought that the less you knew, the safer you'd be."

"And you, Hal? Why the caretaker routine?"

"This is the real me, Casey. I'm a thinker, not a businessman. Playing Hal the caretaker gives me the time and anonymity I need to concentrate on inventions and ideas. Barbara takes care of all the managerial business."

I nodded. I could understand what he meant.

After we'd finished our drinks, Hal said, "I know what you've come to tell us, Jacob, but we have a proposition for you. In the short time you've been with us, we've been impressed by the thoroughness of your work, and we'd like to offer you the position of Head of Research."

Barbara smiled and nodded. "We've talked it over with the rest of the board, and they're in agreement. What do you think?"

"I'm a mathematician, not a research scientist," Dad protested.

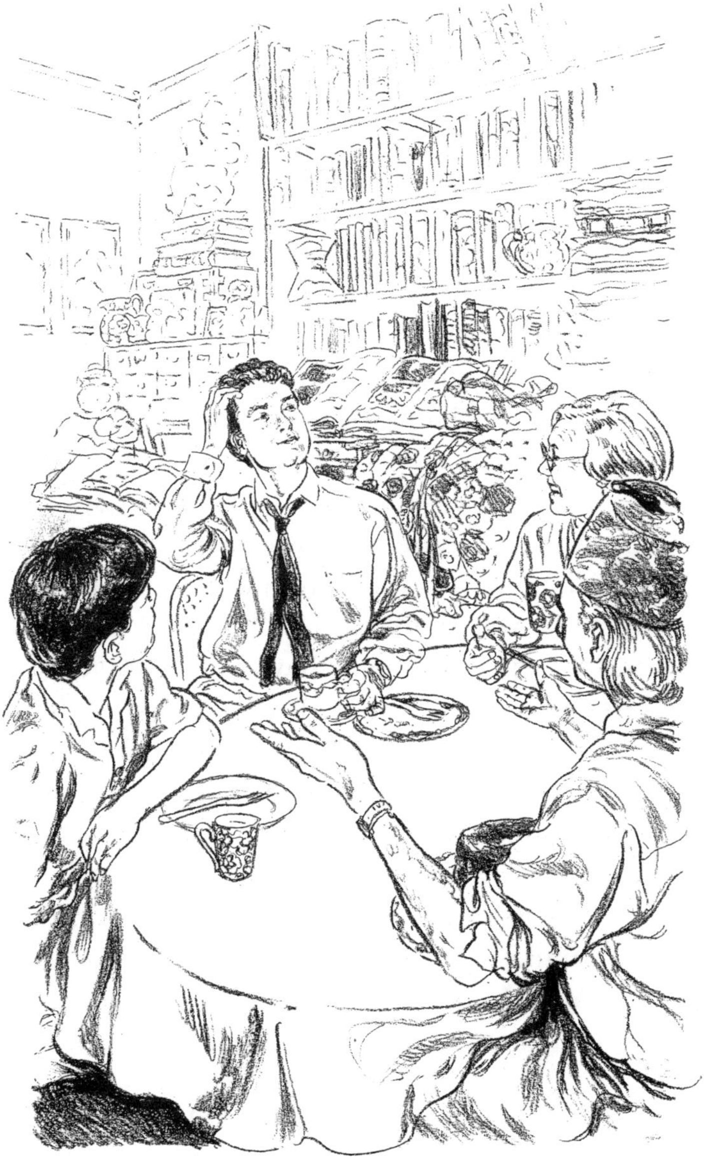

"A brilliant one. I wouldn't ask if I didn't think that you were the best person for the job." Hal smiled.

Dad looked at me, wanting my opinion. I thought for a moment, weighing up the pros and cons. I'd have a permanent home. I'd have Hal and Barbara. And Caroline. In ninety days' time, I'd also have one new, fully-equipped rowing boat, if no one came forward to claim it from the Halls police pound. But, on the other hand, I'd lose my roving lifestyle.

Dad sat, fiddling with his empty cup, twisting it around and around in the saucer. I knew he was thinking that if he took the job and sat still, he'd finally have to face up to the loss of my mother after all these years.

I was a little afraid. Part of me wanted him to say no. Dad looked at me. "Well, Casey, it's crunch time. We've only been here for a short time, but I think we've found a place where both of us could settle for a while. What do you think?"

"Yes," I said, mouthing the word silently.

Unbelievable! The gypsy Sutches were committed.

We were on our way to settling down – whatever that meant – and I only hoped that we wouldn't regret it.

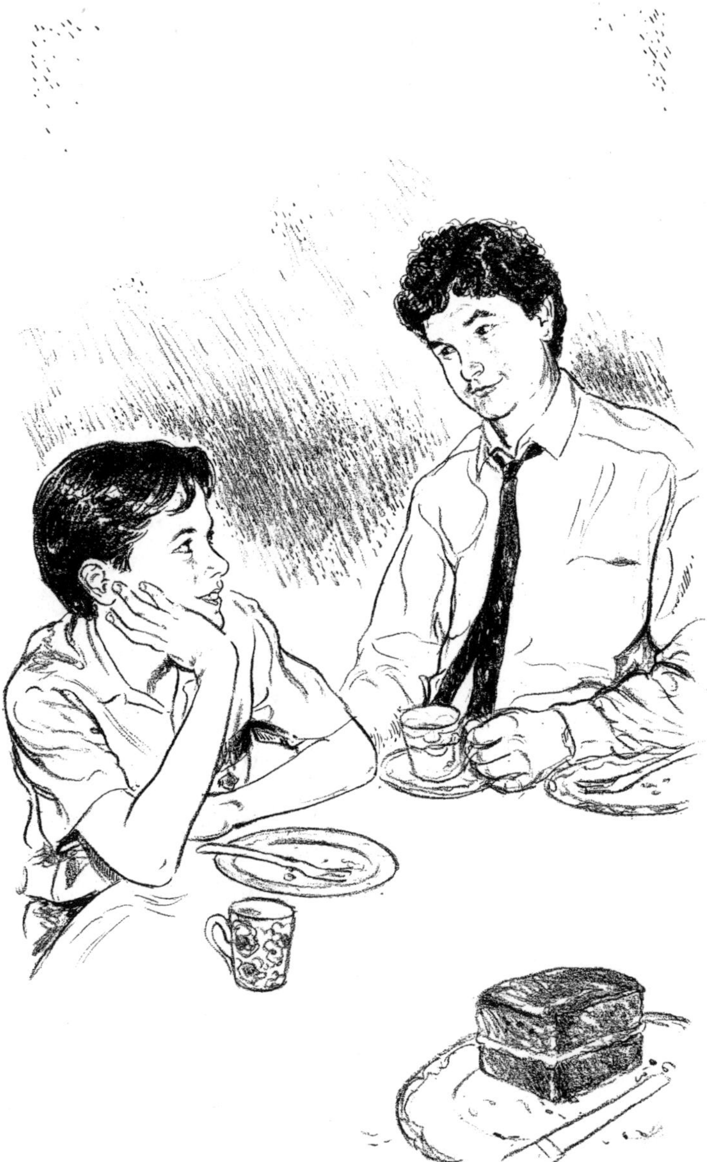

TITLES IN THE SERIES

SET 9A

Television Drama
Time for Sale
The Shady Deal
The Loch Ness Monster Mystery
Secrets of the Desert

SET 9B

To JJ From CC
Pandora's Box
The Birthday Disaster
The Song of the Mantis
Helping the Hoiho

SET 9C

Glumly
Rupert and the Griffin
The Tree, the Trunk, and the Tuba
Errol the Peril
Cassidy's Magic

SET 9D

Barney
Get a Grip, Pip!
Casey's Case
Dear Future
Strange Meetings

SET 10A

A Battle of Words
The Rainbow Solution
Fortune's Friend
Eureka
It's a Frog's Life

SET 10B

The Cat Burglar of Pethaven Drive
The Matchbox
In Search of the Great Bears
Many Happy Returns
Spider Relatives

SET 10C

Horrible Hank
Brian's Brilliant Career
Fernitickles
It's All in Your Mind,
    James Robert
Wing High, Gooftah

SET 10D

The Week of the Jellyhoppers
Timothy Whuffenpuffen-
    Whippersnapper
Timedetectors
Ryan's Dog Ringo
The Secret of Kiribu Tapu Lagoon